Ex Libris

Arlington Garden Club

Arlington, Vermont

VERMONT STATE
SEAL TREE

A Terrarium in your home

William White Jr., Ph.D.
& Sara Jane White

STERLING PUBLISHING CO., INC.   NEW YORK
Oak Tree Press Co., Ltd. London & Sydney

OTHER BOOKS BY THE SAME AUTHOR

The Angelfish: Its Life Cycle
Earthworm Is Born
Edge of the Pond
Forest and Garden

Frog Is Born
The Guppy: Its Life Cycle
The Siamese Fighting Fish: Its Life Cycle
Turtle Is Born

OTHER NATURE BOOKS

Ant Is Born
Bee Is Born
Bird Is Born
Birds That Fly in the Night
Butterfly Is Born
Fern Is Born

Fruit Is Born
Hidden Life of Flowers
The Lobster: Its Life Cycle
The Penguin: Its Life Cycle
Silkworm Is Born
Tree Is Born

The authors and publisher wish to thank William White III and James M. White for their aid in constructing and maintaining the greenhouse and coldframes; Elizabeth J. White and Margaret R. White for many hours of searching for wild plants and flowers in woodlands and fields; Godfrey Ott & Sons of Ott's Exotic Plants, Schwenksville, Penna., and Longwood Gardens, Kennett Square, Penna., for permission to photograph their collections; A. B. Graf for his wise and seasoned views on plant ecology.

Copyright © 1976 by Sterling Publishing Co., Inc.
419 Park Avenue South, New York, N.Y. 10016
Distributed in Australia and New Zealand by Oak Tree Press Co., Ltd.,
P.O. Box J34, Brickfield Hill, Sydney 2000, N.S.W.
Distributed in the United Kingdom and elsewhere in the British Commonwealth
by Ward Lock Ltd., 116 Baker Street, London W 1
Manufactured in the United States of America
All rights reserved
Library of Congress Catalog Card No.: 76-19807
Sterling ISBN 0-8069-3732-7 Trade   Oak Tree 7061-2522-3
3733-5 Library

Contents

Before You Begin 7

1. Selecting a Container 11

2. Preparing the Soil 15
   Planting . . . Care

3. Gathering Plants for the Terrarium 27

4. Light, Temperature and Water 35
   Seasonal Cycles

5. Communities, Synergism and Symbiosis . . . 41

6. Some Native Plants 45
   Algae . . . Fungi . . . Lichens . . . Mosses . . . Ferns
   . . . Small Flowering Plants

7. Plants and Animals 73
   Reptiles and Amphibians

8. History of Terraria 83

Index 92

Illus. 1. A large commercial greenhouse has huge trays used for growing and reproducing ferns and mosses as well as other terrarium plants.

Before You Begin

A terrarium is a miniature indoor garden enclosed in glass, in which various small plants and often small animals are brought together in an artificial environment. It is actually a tiny artificial *biome*, or ecological zone, which you create and maintain yourself.

In order to put together a terrarium that will endure and not die out after a few weeks, you must observe certain rules and understand various natural processes.

First, you must have a proper glass container, one large enough to maintain the artificial balance of life which you seek to establish. Then you must assemble the proper plants and small animals, first making sure that they are not incompatible with or destructive to each other. You can bring plants together in a harmonious grouping that would not be found growing together in nature! But you must also see that they receive the proper care and grow under the conditions that they require.

This book will show you how to create this small world within your own house—a world that will give you great pleasure to watch and which will also give you an opportunity to study the forces of nature close at hand, whatever the weather outside. And on top of that you will

Illus. 2. The author's lean-to greenhouse is made of discarded lumber and an old door and covered with polyethylene sheeting.

have a thing of beauty to adorn your home—a year-round showcase of greenery.

If you thought a terrarium consists of a few little plants crowded into a brandy snifter or a glass bottle, you will gain a different impression from this book.

Start your terrarium career with a small moss garden (see p. 56)—these tiny plants are the easiest to keep and grow and they can be found almost anywhere. When you have achieved success with this you may wish to add a small fern and some lichens. The actual design and layout is completely up to you. You may want to add some stones or even some small animals. The designing of

Illus. 3. In a very large greenhouse gallery, a whole formal garden is grown in the same fashion as the terrarium which can be built and kept at home. This is the large greenhouse of the famed Longwood Gardens in southern Pennsylvania.

terraria and the art of planting them is followed by millions of people of all ages. If you become interested enough in the world of the terrarium, you may want to take the next step and build a simple lean-to greenhouse of scrap timber and polyethylene sheeting. The greenhouse will enable you to maintain your terrarium plants and terraria out of doors during cold weather without having them freeze.

However, building and maintaining a greenhouse is outside the scope of this book. Before you even think of constructing one, be sure that you can maintain a flourishing terrarium.

You may wish to visit one of the large commercial greenhouses and see how they grow and maintain their thousands of plants. They will often welcome your questions and help you solve your problems. There are public horticultural halls in the United States, Canada, Britain and Australia, where you may be able to see whole rooms of giant tree ferns and palms and rain-forest plants festooned with orchids. The important thing to remember is that while the terrarium is a beautiful garden in miniature, it is also a serious scientific tool. You can make your own discoveries. Science can be enjoyable and even beautiful while opening up whole new worlds greater than those of any explorer.

1. Selecting a Container

There are some very definite rules that should be followed in setting up and maintaining a terrarium to insure success.

The choice of a container must be done with consideration not only for the attractiveness and novelty of the container but also for its practicality as a plant environment. Every so many years a different terrarium fad comes into vogue. For this reason some very impractical containers have been displayed in popular magazines, usually showing some hothouse plant that has been put into a wine bottle, apothecary jar or whatever just for the purpose of taking the picture. Many of these novelty arrangements are called "bottle gardens" and are planted with some skill in large water jugs. While a 5-gallon (19-litre) container will work for a few plants it is usually too small and too hard to maintain for animals. Any bottle smaller than this is not practical over any period of time. Other types of glassware, brandy snifters, salad bowls, and such, are woefully inadequate for all but one or two low mosses.

Illus. 4. An old aquarium, purchased cheaply as a "leaker," is used as a woodland terrarium.

Illus. 5. A tiny candy jar used as a moss garden is the smallest kind of practical terrarium.

Almost any clear glass vessel will function as a terrarium. While old bell jars are good, the modern all-glass aquariums are even better. They can be planted with many different plants and are easily large enough in the 10- and 20-gallon (38- and 76-litre) sizes for any of the terrarium animals.

Once the container has been selected, it is necessary to get it thoroughly clean. It should be scrubbed with hot soapy water and some sort of commercial sodium hypochlorite solution such as Clorox®. This will kill most of the moulds which are the constant enemies of terrarium organisms. The next step is to sun-dry the washed enclosure thoroughly and prepare the soil for planting.

Illus. 6. An old piece of wood decays into humus—the fine, powdery soil which is best for terraria.

2. Preparing the Soil

The terrarium, since it assures proper moisture and nourishment, affords an especially lush and rich environment and micro-organisms of all sorts will grow in such an environment far more quickly than in the natural woodland. Therefore, it is necessary that yeasts, moulds, fungus spores and insect eggs and larvae be reduced in the terrarium. There is no practical way to kill or remove them all. Certainly there is no way to eliminate them from the green plants which you intend to grow in your terrarium.

However, the soil must be sterilized as much as is possible. This means that it must be heated. For complete sterilization, the killing of all living organisms, it would have to be heated to over 350°F. (180°C.) and kept at that temperature for three hours—which is obviously not practical. In greenhouses, live steam is often fed through the soil in the plant beds, because moist heat kills microorganisms and invertebrate eggs and young more efficiently than dry heat. With this steam method a temperature of 220°F. (107°C.) may be used for one hour with about the same results.

Illus. 7. The fine dusty soil made by the action of weathering, insects and fungi on this stump, is ideal for terraria.

Since steam is impractical for the home gardener or the student planting a terrarium, it is best to heed the following simple directions:

Planting

1. First, find some thick humus in the woods. The best place is hollow logs and old tree stumps where the insects and fungi have reduced the wood to soft brown sawdust-like material.

2. Place this tree humus in a shallow pan or ceramic container and wrap it in aluminium foil so that any insects contained in it will not escape.

Illus. 8. Humus and sphagnum are cleaned and prepared for the terrarium.

Illus. 9. Long-grained sphagnum moss is packed into the edges and at the base of the terrarium. Sphagnum moss can be obtained from most suppliers.

Illus. 10. Using a small scoop, pick up the humus.

Illus. 11. Sprinkle the humus evenly over the layer of sphagnum already placed on the bottom of the terrarium.

Illus. 12. A suitable clump of moss is cleaned and shaped gently before being placed on top of humus.

Illus. 13. Next the moss is fitted and pressed gently into the place where you want it—remember the layout is your own.

Illus. 14. The humus is pushed around the clump of moss and more humus is added to the cracks between the moss clumps, if needed.

Illus. 15. If wild plants or exotic (house) plants are to be added, a small hole is dug into the humus.

Illus. 16. If the plant you are adding is in a pot (which it will be if it came from a supplier), carefully place the fingers of one hand across the top of the pot, being careful not to crush the little plant.

Illus. 17. Gently invert the pot and tap it smartly on the bottom. This should dislodge the plant and the earth around it cleanly. If this does not work, gently poke the eraser end of a pencil through the drainage hole and push.

21

Illus. 18. Gently lift up the inverted pot, which should come away clean.

Illus. 19. Next the plant, with the earth from the pot clinging to its roots, is pressed carefully into the hole, and humus is pushed into place around it.

3. Bake the wrapped humus in a standard oven at 250°F. (120°C.) for 90 minutes or more. Remove from the oven and cool.

4. Sift the baked and cooled humus by rubbing it over a wire mesh of the size used to control mosquitoes, the type mounted in ordinary window screens. This will yield a fine brown soil.

5. Place the soil in the clean, dry terrarium enclosure.

6. Select plants with a fair amount of root-stock and plant them in the humus, making sure that they are placed at the proper soil depth—in other words, that they are not higher above the soil level than they would be in nature. Water the plants gently with a sprinkler or sprayer. Do not pour the water on them and do not press down the soil around them.

7. Place a tight glass top over the terrarium. You can have this cut to size from window glass.

8. Wait until the plants are established for several weeks before introducing any animals.

Care

1. Although the terrarium must have moisture, it must not have too much. Feel the soil along the inside of the glass to see if it is dry at all. If so, water until it is moist but not clay-like. The glass sides should be misty from transpiration after some hours in the sun. If not, then the terrarium is not receiving sufficient water. If any

of the soil surface looks moist and stays that way, it is probably too wet.

2. As the plants grow, some may become too large. These should be removed or trimmed to prevent the smaller plants from being choked off or prevented from getting sufficient light. If you include oak seedlings (see p. 72) in your plant material, these will die if pinched back or trimmed, but other woodland plants can be trimmed back. When the oak seedlings grow too big, simply remove them carefully.

3. Plants which suffer severe insect infestations can be washed with mild soapy water—in cases of very severe infestation the leaves and stems can be swabbed with alcohol. If the plant has started to wilt or droop from the infestation, it is better to discard it than to risk the infestation of any other of your plants. To wash plants, wet a small sponge with mild, soapy water and gently sponge the leaves only.

4. With care the terrarium should only require 6 to 8 hours of light per day. However, this must be the right type of light. If artificial illumination is used it should be a fluorescent light made specifically for growing plants and be plugged into an automatic timer. No matter how dedicated a plant raiser you may be, it is simply impossible to provide the specific timing

of light available with an inexpensive timer. Check with a plant supply shop as to where to obtain proper lighting and timer.

5. A well settled terrarium will do very well, since the plants manufacture their own food through photosynthesis. If the plants lose their color or begin to droop, change the lighting or add more water, but do not use chemical fertilizers. These are too rich and there are simply not enough outlets for the excess food—it will only feed unwanted parasites and moulds.

Illus. 20. In the desert environment of northern Mexico, cactus plants sprout from the hot, dry sand and gravel.

Illus. 21. The stone plant is another herb characteristic of the dry desert biome. Like the cactus it has thick porous tissues to conserve water.

3. Gathering Plants for the Terrarium

The earth has a number of different types of climates in which many types of plants grow. The most important ones as sources of house plants are the desert, the rain-forest and the temperate woodland. Plants from all three areas are kept in houses and gardens. The three aspects of a single plant area, that is, the climate conditions plus the soil plus the range of plants of the region constitute a *biome*. Thus, there is: a desert biome, a rain-forest biome and a woodland biome.

The desert biome has a very low humidity, oftentimes it may not rain but once or twice a year! It has sandy soil and lots of stones and rocks. There is bright, hot sunshine every day of the year. The major danger to the plants of the desert biome is drought, drying up in the heat. The plants are solid and compact with thick leaves and stems in which water can be collected and stored. Because these conditions of heat and sun are so basic, the plants and their life cycles are adapted to fit the conditions. There are

Illus. 22. A tropical orchid grows from the thin soil of the rain-forest.

many kinds of plants that have these adaptations but the most common and most popular are the cactus species. They must be kept in warm dry environments and cannot be kept in an enclosed terrarium.

The rain-forest biome is marked by heat and humidity. The soil is shallow and of poor quality and the trees shade the ground until it is almost like night in the underbrush. Many of the smaller plant species actually grow on or climb up the trees to get some sunlight. The chief danger to the growth of plants in the rain-forest is the threat of drowning in seasonal floods. The seeds must be large and water-resistant. Among the commonest rain-forest plant species are the many thousands of kinds of orchids. The

Illus. 23. There are some 15,000 varieties of orchids of every shape and size growing mostly in the rain-forests of the world. A few species can be found in the temperate woodland. However, be sure first that they are not protected by law before you dig any up.

rain-forest plants are often kept in terraria with some shade and lots of water and organic material. They must be kept warm, moist and away from drafts, and growing most of them, especially orchids, is beyond the scope of this book.

For our purposes, the most suitable plants are those of the temperate woodlands. The woodland biome, the environment of the temperate regions of the world, is the one that is dominated by the leaf-dropping or deciduous trees which lose their leaves each autumn and grow new ones each spring. The chief features of the woodland biome are the changing of the seasons and the incredibly

Illus. 24. A woodland along a ridge in the Appalachian uplands is covered with deciduous trees which will drop their leaves in the autumn.

rich soil made up of the humus or decayed matter from the leaf-falls of previous seasons. It is the cooling of the air and the freezing of the water supply in the form of ice and snow which presents the greatest danger to the woodland plants. Most simply die back above ground, like the ferns, and regrow their green fronds in the spring. The woodland plants have complicated life cycles which match the change of seasons and the variations in the amount of water available.

The woodland plants which are the most attractive and interesting for the terrarium can either be found by searching for them in the woods, or many of them can

Illus. 25. The cycle of humification is basic to the growth of the ferns and other small plants in the woodland. Here a stump is being reduced to basic organic materials by fungi and insects.

also be purchased from plant dealers and greenhouse growers. Since it is necessary to have small plants in the terrarium, not all woodland plants are good for the terrarium. No one wants a Jack-in-the-Beanstalk type of plant growing through the roof of his home. The fact is, many woodland plants stay small because there are natural limits on their growth—the supplies of light, water and nutrients are limited by the woodland environment itself. Not only must the terrarium provide the needed requirements but it must also provide them in just the proper amounts to limit the growth of the plants. These requirements are fertile, pest-free soil, a half-day of light, enough

Illus. 26. In the shadow of a rotted log, nuts and seeds germinate, many of them collected and buried there by forgetful squirrels.

water to keep the soil just moist and a community of those micro-organisms that are beneficial to the soil.

It is almost possible to say that some plants in the woodland give up the choice of competing with the trees by growing big, and instead stay small in a less hospitable environment where the competition is less and the chance of successful growth and reproduction is much greater. These include the lichens, mosses, ferns and small flowering plants. These little plants need less light—in fact, many cannot survive long exposure to direct sunlight because they would soon dry up and die, through the process called desiccation. Because they cannot tolerate the harsher conditions of the open field, they must have richer soil and more nutrients. They must have the shade of the taller trees and the moisture that the shade helps to provide and the humus which collects on the forest floor.

Humus is built up year by year by the action of a whole series of organisms as they break down the cellulose, the basic plant material of the fallen leaves, and convert it into foodstuffs and minerals. These organisms include bacteria, earthworms, springtail insects and more bacteria. The dark layer of sour-smelling, soft brown humus can be found

Illus. 27. The woodland has three layers of growth, the trees, the ground-cover and the humus-loving plants. Here the ground-cover almost obscures the humus and the smaller plants beneath.

Illus. 28. A slanting ray of sunshine illuminates the ground and small plants at the base of a large deciduous tree. Note the fallen leaves from the preceding season.

below the layer of leaves under almost any forest tree. It is within this layer that the spores and seeds of the ground plants, the lichens, mosses, ferns and tiny wildflowers thrive.

4. Light, Temperature and Water

While the forest plants may get some hours of direct sunlight each day, it is usually not while the sun is high in the sky, but at early morning and late evening just before sunset. The only time and place that they do get the full sun's rays are during the winter months, when the trees are leafless, and in high mountainous or Alpine environments. While many people think of woodland plants as needing warmth, this is not actually true. The tiny lichens are so resistant to cold that they are the only plants which can grow in the Arctic and are frequently found on glaciers. The mosses and ferns can also withstand bitter cold that would freeze many other types of plants to death. As long as the freezing does not prevent the roots from getting water, it will not hurt the woodland plants. Many varieties of woodland plants thrive under the fallen leaves and snow throughout the winter. They are almost the first green plants to appear in the spring.

Illus. 29. As autumn progresses into winter, the edges of a swamp show the bare stems of plants which have lost their leaves. Many of the bog plants have receded back into the mud beneath the water's edge where they will remain dormant until spring.

In the woodland the light reaching the plants below the trees is often diffuse, which means that it is already weak because it has passed through the leaves and branches of the tall trees which shadow the undergrowth. While the larger and broader ferns are very attractive, they are also more likely to outgrow their quarters. The art of keeping plants small while allowing them to grow and complete their life cycle is very ancient and was brought to perfection in the Orient thousands of years ago. The dwarfing is done by restricting the amount of light and water the plant receives and constricting it in a small container.

Illus. 30. An ancient tree dwarfed into a tiny pot by skilfully depriving it of all but the barest nutrients. Such a tree passes through all the seasonal changes. Here it has dropped its leaves, and may have been dropping them for several hundred years!

To keep terrarium plants compact, the top leaves and buds should be cut back. With care, you can also uproot the plant and trim the roots. Side shoots growing from the stem can also be clipped to promote compact side growth. Most electric light, whether incandescent or fluorescent, is not suffused enough, since it comes from above, or from one direction. Plants grown in such light are always growing toward the source of light and tend to become stalky. Unless you have special lighting arrangements that will provide suffused light, natural sunlight is preferable, since it produces more compact plants.

Illus. 31. A slowly decaying stump is caught in the grip of a heavy frost. Such frosts, which mark the end of the growing season in the temperate zone, delay the process of reduction which goes on inside the dead wood and rotting roots.

Seasonal Cycles

If the woodland plants pass through a seasonal cycle, it is best that they pass through a similar cycle in the terrarium. This means that the temperature changes of the seasons must be followed in the terrarium. The one exception is the freezing cold of winter. The terrarium and its plants can be cooled but must be kept from freezing. At the other extreme, the terrarium must be shaded and kept cool during the summer to simulate the action of the trees in the woods. Plants in a terrarium give off a large amount of water vapor through a process

Illus. 32. A commercial plastic terrarium displays transpiration mist covering its sides.

Illus. 33. The frozen ground of the forest, covered by the new leaf fall, receives the first snowfall of winter. This is the harshest season which the woodland must survive.

Illus. 34. A spring-side brook babbles over stones. Along such brooks, a wealth of terrarium plants can be found, including lichens, mosses and ferns.

called transpiration. This water collects on the sides of the terrarium in the form of drops. Because plants recycle water in this fashion, it is unnecessary to water a well-balanced terrarium. In fact the most common failure people have with woodland plants is caused by "killing them with kindness." They give them too much sunlight, water them too often and give them chemical fertilizers which are too strong for them to utilize.

5. Communities, Synergism and Symbiosis

Many kinds of plants live together in nature in a sort of co-operative arrangement or community. In a way, the whole forest is such a community, in fact the community of trees, plants, and animals *is* the forest. The oak tree, the squirrel and the soil bacteria are all components of the forest. No one of them could exist without all of the others being in their places and working in the system. The most interesting aspect of the whole forest is the flow of energy through and to all of its components. The energy comes from the sun in the form of what is called radiation.

There are many kinds of radiation including heat, light and sound. The radiation used by the green matter or chlorophyll in plants is the orange-red and blue light of the spectrum. But not all of the energy used by the woodland plants of any one season comes directly from the sun. Some of it was captured and stored in chemical compounds by previous generations of plants. The fungi and bacteria of the forest use this energy stored in dead plants to support themselves. Even the green plants must have a large number of minerals and organic compounds to survive and most of these are released by decay from the energy stored up by previous generations of plants.

The energy cycle is basic to forest life. When two different organisms utilize the flow of energy for their own advantage so that the energy, in effect, does double the work, it is called *synergism*. The woodland is one enormous process of synergism. It uses and reuses the same trapped sun energy to grow trees, enable squirrels to climb, provide flight for insects, give sound to bird songs and then, finally, to reduce its own dead materials and wastes. The same processes take place, on a much smaller scale, in the terrarium. The woodland, or one tiny segment of it, in the terrarium is a marvellous synergism. It is worth every moment spent to observe and understand it.

Plants can aid each other in other ways than in the flow and use of energy. Many smaller plants of the woodland will grow up or climb up the bark of trees to get above the ground-cover and obtain more sunlight. Such "growing-on-taller-plant" species are called *epiphytes*. All vines are epiphytes, as they grow up tall trees and rocks to search out the sun. Other plant species live in such close relationship that they actually appear to be one species. The lichen is the best example as it is really two plants, an alga and a fungus colony growing together for the mutual benefit of both. This shared benefit relationship is called *symbiosis*. It is always worth the effort to observe which

Illus. 35. A tropical epiphyte grows high up on the bark of a rain-forest tree to seek more light and rainfall.

Illus. 36. Two types of plants living in association—ferns and lichens. The rocks are covered with lichens which will help in time to split the rocks and release their mineral contents. The ferns are growing and spreading in the humus-rich soil between the cracked rocks.

Illus. 37. An assortment of mosses and other small woodland plants await placement in a terrarium.

plants seem to grow together in the woods and to put them together in the terrarium.

Some plants actually prevent other plants from growing near them, and this is called *antagonism*. There is no point in putting antagonistic species together in the same enclosure. For example, plants of the buttercup family are often poisonous to other plants. This family includes such woodland plants as columbines, marsh marigolds, anemones and hepaticas. In general, you will do best to follow the rule of choosing those plants that you find growing together in the woods. There are various popular books on gardening that touch on this subject.*

---

*One is Audrey Wynne Hatfield's *How to Enjoy Your Weeds*, Sterling.

6. Some Native Plants

Any terrarium can be planted with either native plants which grow right around your own home or locality or with exotic plants which are grown by greenhouse growers and which you can buy. It is usually better to try and find your own plants. For one thing, you will learn more about them and where and how they grow in their woodland environment if you go out and look for them. You will also find that not many greenhouses or plant stores grow the native plants. In many cases, the native plants are rarer and more desirable than the ones grown for sale.

There are six basic kinds of plants which can be found in the woodland and can be grown in the terrarium. Each is worth consideration and a try at growing.

Algae

The green algae are the simplest green plants. They are able to manufacture their own foodstuffs from water, carbon dioxide and sunlight. In other words they are self-sustaining or *autotrophic*. They are one-celled but when

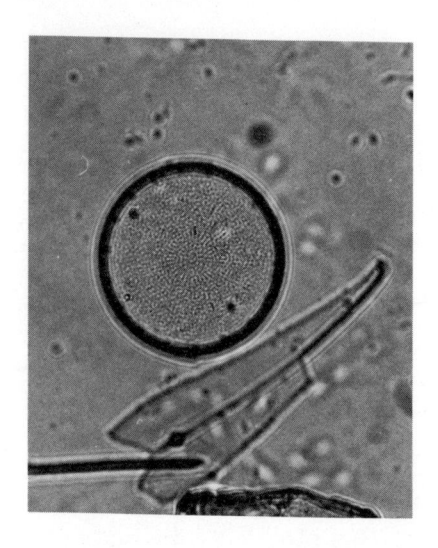

Illus. 38. Pieces and parts of diatoms and other single-celled algae can be found in the wetter portions of almost any terrarium but require high magnification to see. 440X

provided with enough organic material and minerals will grow so luxuriantly that they are easily seen. They form a green scum found on almost all ponds and lakes. They are the green plants which make the ocean look green near the shores of all continents. They are always present in any wet terrarium. They will grow along the sides where the water condenses from vapor and runs down the glass forming tiny puddles all around the margins of the terrarium. They reproduce by simple fission, dividing down the middle. They are the chief source of food in all bodies of water and supply the trapped energy of the sun to many other organisms. They are the bottom link in the distribution of sun energy in the food chain.

Illus. 39. A filamentous alga forms the green scum and coating which cover the margins of almost all bodies of water. 440X

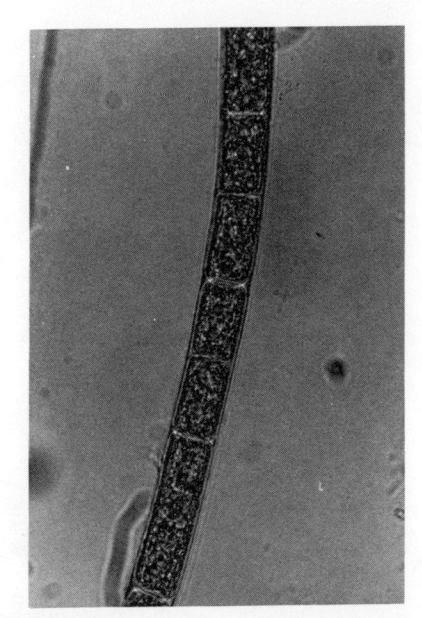

Fungi

The fungi are plants which feed on dead organic material. For this reason they are called "dead-eaters" or *saprophytes*. The most familiar fungi are mushrooms and moulds. However, they come in a whole range of sizes, shapes and colors. They have no true roots but send fine filaments of protoplasm into the dead plants, tree trunks and animals upon which they feed. Through these filaments, called *hyphae*, they secrete chemicals called *hormones* which dissolve the hardest of woods and the toughest of plant fibres so that they can be utilized as food by the fungus. Most fungi reproduce by simply growing from the hyphae or by spore formation. Although they are not usually planted or grown in terrariums, they are almost

Illus. 40. Fungi occur in many shapes and colors in the woodlands. Here a dead tree is being reduced by bracket fungi. Small growths of fungi will appear in shaded terrarium settings, sprung from spores brought in with woodland plant material.

always present on dead wood or in the woodland humus. If the terrarium is placed in a dark place and kept moist they will almost always begin to grow and thrive. A fungi terrarium is one type that is very well worth trying to maintain. Algae and fungi can combine into a specific organism with the best adaptations of both, the lichen.

You can make a fungi terrarium in the following way:

1. First find some well rotted dead branches and place them in the terrarium.
2. Locate the fungi and remove them *with* the material in or on which they are growing.

Illus. 41. A peculiar saprophyte, the Indian pipe, grows in wet woodlands from dead materials buried in the humus. On occasion, these pale white stalks can be transplanted to terraria. Although they can be mistaken for fungi, they are really degenerate flowering plants.

3. Place the fungus material on the dead wood.
4. Place the terrarium in a cool, dark place.
5. Keep terrarium very moist and add new rotted wood or clean compost every two weeks.
6. Then watch new moulds and fungi appear and grow.

Lichens

Lichens often appear as the crusty paint-like patches that grow on trees or on bare rocks. They are very well suited to the harsh environment of bare rock. They are one of the most perfect of *symbionts* (organisms living in symbiosis). The outer layer of fungus provides a tough coating which resists drying and is nearly impossible to freeze. It also secretes hormones of such strength that they actually etch and crack the rocks on which they cling. If

Illus. 42. These rocks resting in a shallow stream by the shore of an Appalachian lake, are covered with crustose lichens looking like layers of greenish-white paint. In time, these small symbionts made up of a colony of algae wrapped in a colony of fungi, will break up the rocks on which they live.

Illus. 43. The leaf-like thallus of a lichen is a layer of transparent fungus containing the cells of algae. 40X

Illus. 44. The red crest or British soldier lichen is found in almost any wooded area and can easily be spotted since the tiny caps turn a deep scarlet in cold weather. These tiny symbionts do very well in the terrarium.

water runs into the cracks and freezes, it may expand and break the rock. The algae cells inside the fungus can carry on photosynthesis and produce foodstuffs for themselves and the outer coating of fungus. This unusual cooperation is so successful that lichens live in most of the inaccessible places on earth. They thrive on the tops of high mountains, and on the Arctic snows and glaciers. They are easy to find and fascinating to grow in terraria.

Illus. 45. Pyxie cups, which are the caps of the fruticose goblet lichen, are easily found in bare patches of rock and do well in terraria.

Lichens reproduce when they produce small pieces containing both alga cells and a few hyphae. These may be carried off by the wind or washed away by floods. When they alight on a new spot where there is enough sun they begin to grow. These little pieces are called *sporedia* and are as fine as dust. Once in a while the fungus part of the lichen will form spores by itself. However, unless these can find the right type of algae where they land, no new lichen will be able to grow. Lichens come in many colors and appear as crusty or leaf-like patches, whose lobes are called *thalli*.

To grow lichens in a terrarium, first put the rock, piece of bark or dead branch on which the lichen is growing into the terrarium. Keep it fairly moist and in direct sunlight. If additional stones and pieces of dead wood are added, the lichens will spread to them. The only real problem is keeping the lichens cool, especially in a heated house in winter. In summer keep them in a cool place, covered. In winter they can usually be left outside with the terrarium cover off.

Mosses

The mosses are small rootless plants which cover the earth under nearly every forest tree and are also found around gutters, cisterns, outbuildings, and other damp places. They consist of tiny leaves which carry on a great

Illus. 46. The gametophytes (sexual stage) of the club moss grow through a carpet of fallen leaves.

Illus. 47. Close-up of the gametophyte stage of the common club moss.

Illus. 48. Pale green Victoria moss is often seen in large public greenhouse displays.

Illus. 49. The sporophyte (asexual stage) capsules of a moss are about to open and release clouds of spores.

amount of photosynthesis, the process of turning the basic gases and minerals into food. Mosses spread over almost any surface and add a bright green color to the forest floor. They reproduce in two different stages, unlike the

Illus. 50. Low-spreading Irish moss *(Selaginella krausiana denticulata)* is widely used in terrarium plantings and can be found or purchased in many varieties.

55

Illus. 51. (Left) A discarded powder box with a transparent plastic top can be used to house a moss garden. (Right) The mosses within the tiny box.

algae—that is, they alternate between asexual generations, which spread by growing up from underground shoots, and sexual generations which produce two types of reproductive cells, male and female. The male cells produce sperm, which must have water surrounding them in order that they can swim over to the female cells and bring about fertilization and the development of spores. Spores are tiny, nearly microscopic cells which can start new moss plants somewhere else. Mosses are very easy to find and should be the basic plant type in any terrarium. In lifting them from the spot where you find them, try also to remove some of the bark, humus or decaying wood on which they are growing. Their tiny spore cases or capsules will grow to maturity in the terrarium and pop open to release thousands of spores to keep the colony growing.

Illus. 52. In a sort of symbiosis, the low-lying moss retains the moisture on the ground which the fern requires in order to reproduce and grow, while the fern maintains the shade required by the mosses.

Ferns

The ferns are the most extensive group of plants kept in terraria. They range from tiny green spots only a few fractions of an inch across to gigantic tree-like plants 60 or more feet (19 metres) in height. The ferns of the temperate woodlands die back each autumn and lie under the leaf mulch and the snow in the form of curled stems. These stems unfurl in the spring as the familiar "fiddle heads" or *croziers*. Ferns are among the most easily found plants and by far the largest which reproduce by spores. Like the mosses, all ferns pass through two alternate

Illus. 53. A patch of ruffled ferns will grow in profusion and continue to reproduce year after year if provided with humus, shade and sufficient moisture.

Illus. 54. The most common type of fern frond or leaf has individual palm-like pinnules or leaflets.

Illus. 55. The less common maiden-hair fern has leaf-like fronds, grows much fuller and closer to the ground and is therefore a highly desired terrarium specimen.

Illus. 56. A gigantic tropical fern shows the crozier or "fiddle head" as a new frond uncoils from the heart of the plant.

Illus. 57. A large maiden-hair fern bears sori on the edges of the leaflets.

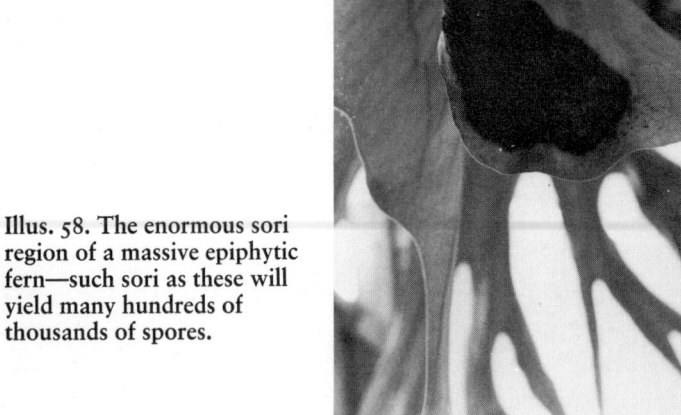

Illus. 58. The enormous sori region of a massive epiphytic fern—such sori as these will yield many hundreds of thousands of spores.

Illus. 59. A microscopic view of the leaf of a fern shows the spore cases or sacs hanging below. 40X

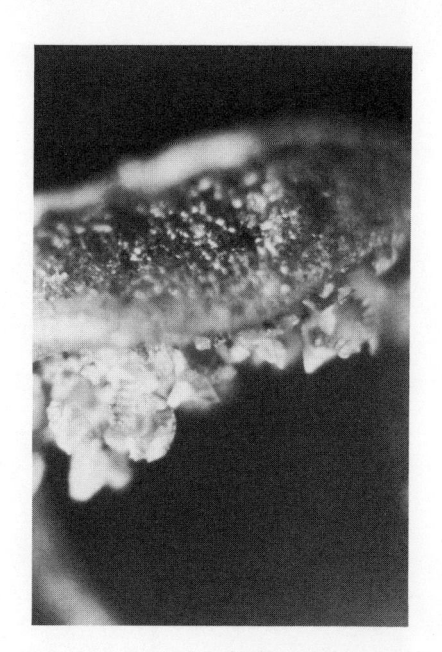

generations. The one is the familiar large, frond-like leaf form called the *sporophyte*, which has the brown *sori* or spore organs on the undersides of its leaves. The other is the tiny sexual form, the *gametophyte*, which may be either male or female. These two generations alternate from season to season.

The spores of ferns can be collected and grown. They differ from seeds in three respects. First, they are very much smaller, usually invisible without a microscope. Secondly, they have no protective seed coats, and thirdly, they contain no pre-packed foodstuffs like those of a bean

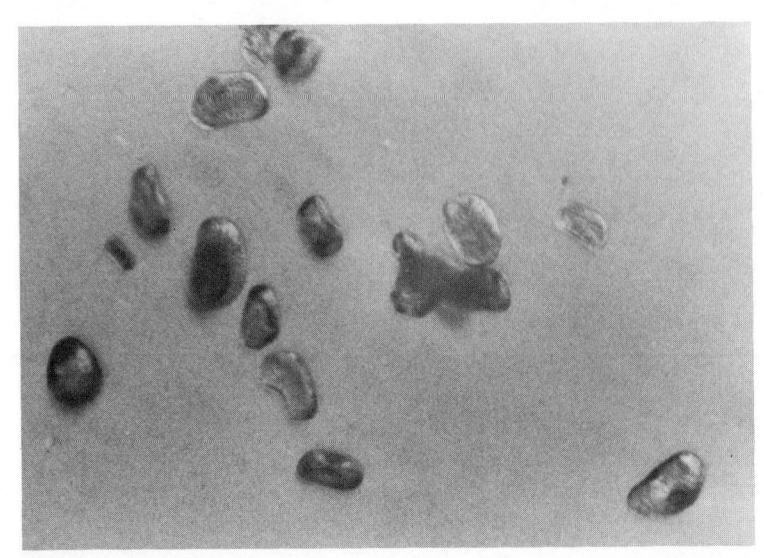

Illus. 60. The spores of a fern are tiny germ cells which have no stored food as do seeds and nuts and therefore must germinate and begin to photosynthesize almost immediately in order to survive. 100X

Illus. 61. An old moss-covered log has been reduced to pure humus. On the surface are the young sporophytes of some species of fern and the tiny, mature gametophytes of others.

Illus. 62. Floating ferns are tropical but are sometimes kept in aquaria and do well in shallow water dishes in terraria. Water dishes should be only one inch (2.5 cm.) deep and 6 inches (15 cm.) or more across. The species shown here is *Salvinia rotundifolia,* the floating moss fern.

seed or an acorn. The spore must germinate on a suitable living surface or perish. Ferns do exceedingly well in the continuous humidity and confined space of the terrarium. It is fascinating to take the sori from under the leaves of a sporophyte and place them on a wet piece of blotting paper or filter paper and see them grow. This can be done with care and a good magnifying glass as a side project of terrarium management.

Another group of non-flowering plants are the horsetails, which share many of the characteristics of ferns, but less variety of form and habit.

Illus. 63. The floating mosquito fern *(Azolla caroliniana)* often gives a green or reddish color to the margins of still-water ponds in tropical climates in North America.

Illus. 64. Thin fern-like spikes typify the ancient tribe of horsetails, a group of plants resembling ferns. They make good terrarium plants, but you will not find them at plant dealers'. You will have to look around in the woods.

Illus. 65. The rattlesnake plantain grows from a thick root called a rhizome. This species does very well in the terrarium and is one of the real prizes of the wild plant collector.

Small Flowering Plants

The flowering plants or *angiosperms* are the most common types of plants known to gardeners and farmers. They include most of our common plants and trees other than ferns and conifers—from the mighty oak to the shrinking violet. There are many small species which grow in the woodland and are very suitable for the terrarium. These are shade-loving and require a good moisture content. Many compete with the trees which usually shade them by blooming early in the spring before the

Illus. 66. There are many, many different plants of the family Marantaceae. They are tropical in origin but widely grown and sold for rain-forest terraria. They grow well if they get sunlight and a lot of moisture. Seen here are typical plants of the genus Maranta.

Illus. 67. The episcia, a relative of the gloxinia, comes from Colombia, and is a creeping vine-like plant. It can be grown from cuttings as well as from seed and produces beautiful orange to yellow flowers. It requires water and shade.

Illus. 68. Pileas are relatives of the nettle. This species, called the "Pan-American friendship plant," comes from Peru. It grows well in the shady terrarium but the new growth at the ends of the stems must be pinched off and discarded to keep the plant low-growing.

shrubs and trees have come into full leaf. Many exotic flowering plants from other woodland areas of the world are stocked by greenhouse growers and listed in many mail-order catalogues. However, the buyer should always look up each species in a good garden or plant book and learn their characteristics before buying.

Among exotic plants that make good terrarium dwellers are marantas, pileas, episcias, podocarpus, ficus, and cryptanthus, many of which are grown for their attractive foliage as much as for their flowers.

Illus. 69. The podocarpus or ming tree is one of the few evergreens related to the pines and firs that are kept in terraria. It came originally from China and can withstand colder temperatures.

Illus. 70. The cryptanthus is a relative of the pineapple plant that can live for years with little care in terraria. It is tropical and many species are epiphytes.

Illus. 71. The ficus or "creeping fig," a low-growing vine from China and Japan, climbs by its roots, withstands some cold and grows very well in terraria.

A unique group of small angiosperms which do very well in the terrarium are the carnivorous plants such as sundew and Venus's fly-trap. They live in bogs which have low nitrogen levels in the soil. They are usually grown from bulbs and can be kept in a warm and wet terrarium. They will usually trap flies or small beetles that are placed on their modified leaves called traps. Once caught, the insects are dissolved by powerful enzymes secreted by the plant. The nitrogen is absorbed from the insect and the hard outer shell allowed to decay through bacterial action or dumped out of the trap after absorption.

Illus. 72. There are many types of pitcher plants from all over the world, but they all come from bogs where the nitrogen content of the soil is low. They are carnivorous, capturing insects in their bottle-like pitchers. Special leaves lined with waxy scales and hairy projections allow insects in but will not permit them to climb back out until they are digested by powerful enzymes. This specimen is a fascinating little pitcher plant from Australia—*Cephalotis follicularis.*

The best angiosperms, like the best ferns, are the ones that you find yourself. However, you must be very careful not to remove wild plants from areas where they are protected. Many horticultural societies and garden clubs maintain protected areas. But if you look long enough and carefully enough you will be amazed at how many very desirable species you can find. Remember that many wild species grow from thick running roots called *rhizomes.*

Illus. 73. The Venus's-flytrap is a native American wild bog plant with an ingenious adaptation. Each leaf is folded in half and has teeth-like fringes on the edges. The plant gives off a sour smell which attracts flies. When a fly steps into the leaves, they close and trap the insect, whose soft parts are then digested. The dried shell or carapace is later dropped out when the leaf re-opens.

With care and attention, most wild plants can be grown from just a few inches of rhizome.

Although not properly terrarium plants, trees, or at least the seedlings of trees, can be germinated and raised in terraria. Since the seeds of most upland deciduous trees germinate and grow in shade and considerable moisture in the forest humus, they can be given the same conditions for germination and growth in the terrarium as small woodland plants.

Illus. 74. A mixed terrarium with native American mosses and an exotic pitcher plant. Although these plants would never occur growing together in nature, they do very well in the terrarium. The possible combinations are unlimited and anyone can try new ones.

Tree seedlings, of course, cannot be expected to remain in the terrarium indefinitely. Maple seedlings can be kept for about one year, others for two years, such as oak. Most tree seedlings can be clipped back, with the notable exception of oak.

Among the woodland herbs that can be gathered in eastern North America for use in terraria are cobra lilies, pipsissewa, rattlesnake plantain, wood-sorrel, spiderwort, violets, wintergreen, wild strawberry, pussy toes, lungwort, bearberry, buckbean, sanicle, and Solomon's seal.

7. Plants and Animals

The 18th-century chemist Joseph Priestley discovered that a plant would provide life-supporting gas for a rat when both were enclosed in a large bell jar. Another Englishman, Nathaniel Ward, discovered that the gas exhaled by the animal was used by the plant and that the gas produced by the plant was used by the animal. This was the principle of the balanced plant-animal community of the terrarium or aquarium. In theory, the plants could use the animal waste as fertilizer and the animal could feed on the plant. But this is just theory. In fact, there would never be enough plants in any conveniently small enclosure to feed an animal or animal community.

It would be impossible to have a closed terrarium in which the animals would depend on the plants for food and the plants on the animals for fertilizer. In only a few generations, which would be only a few months with some species of insects, there would be no more plants to be eaten. However, it is possible to keep some kinds of very small animals in terraria if the system is not closed—if, that is, food is added for the animals and they are not expected to eat the plants.

Illus. 75. An anole (American chameleon) hunts insects in the mosses of a terrarium with the cunning and skill of a tiger in the jungle.

Reptiles and Amphibians

There are a number of animals which will do very well in a terrarium and the best are either reptiles or amphibians. The common garden or woods toad, an amphibian, will live in a terrarium throughout the winter. It should be fed live insects such as the commercial meal worms sold in pet shops. One small toad will not dig up the plants enough to destroy them, although it will probably dig a burrow if the soil is deep enough (about 3 inches or 7.5 cm.). If you plan to keep a toad, see that there is plenty of moss, as this is best for the toad to burrow under.

Another animal which is very suitable is the anole, the green lizard sold in pet shops under the name "chameleon" (the true chameleon actually comes from Africa). The anole, which occurs in almost all areas of the southeastern United States, will live for years in captivity if properly cared for. Anoles live in woodlands and feed on insects, such as flies and crickets, once a week. They lay large eggs in mulch, usually six to a dozen in a clutch. These eggs hatch during the first hot weather of the season. Anoles are difficult to breed in captivity but will take up territories. That is, each anole will select an area of about 16 square inches (105 cm. sq.), from which it will drive off other animals.

Another suitable reptile is the small box turtle. Although box turtles are very difficult to find in the woods, they can be found occasionally and do well in captivity with careful attention to their needs. Their needs are food, soft soil to hide in and privacy—they do not like being prodded, fondled or teased. A 2-inch (5-cm.) box turtle in an indoor terrarium requires $1\frac{1}{2}$ square feet (0.135 m. sq.) of territory. Box turtles should be put out of doors in an enclosure for the summer and when they grow larger. They will dig under the plants and must be provided with some dense plant growths. They need sunlight but cannot tolerate too much humid heat. Heat and humidity can be regulated by leaving the cover off the terrarium and by

Illus. 76. A young box turtle makes its way through the grass of an enclosure.

limiting sprinkling to once a week. Their diet should include lettuce, carrots, fruits, berries and ground beef. The box turtle lays eggs in the forest mulch in a sunny spot and these can be incubated in captivity. Toads and box turtles can be kept in the same terrarium if they are about equal in size.

Less obvious but even more important as terrarium animals are the insects. While most gardeners do all they can to rid their plants of insects, the terrarium is an especially fine place to keep and study them. You will need a small magnifier of at least 10× power to see the eggs and moulting stages of most of the tiny insects and arachnids which are part of every terrarium. Surprisingly enough, while many thousands of different products are sold to control and kill insects on household plants, few

Illus. 77. The semicircle of eggs laid by the white fly. These purplish eggs stand on fine stalks, which are formed from a secretion exuded by the body of the adult white fly.

people know much about the incredible life cycles of their insect pests. If the terrarium is to be more than an ornament, it must be a laboratory for science, and a tool of discovery.

Three small insects are almost universal on plants whether in terraria, pots or out of doors. One of these is the white fly, a small white moth-like insect which lays its purple eggs on stalk-like appendages in a characteristic half-moon pattern. These develop and hatch into small white-yellowish caterpillars that ravage plants by actually eating the leaves and sucking juices.

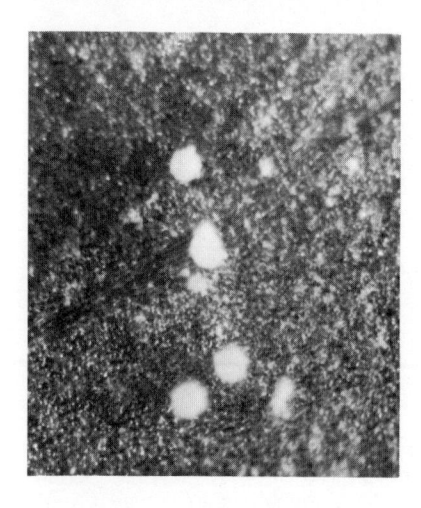

Illus. 78. The mealy larvae of the white fly are sucking the plant juices from the leaves.

Another plant insect is the springtail. These are very primitive wingless insects with two large flaps sticking out beyond the tail. When threatened, the springtail can bound many times its length of only about 1/25th of an inch (1 mm.) by springing on its tail flaps. Springtails play a very important part in the humification cycle and they are obtainable from almost any tiny plant pot. The easiest way to find them is to take a small piece of rotten wood from the ground and slap it hard against a piece of newspaper. The tiny ant-like creatures that will run out are springtails. They can be further identified by poking them gently with a pencil point or pin point—if they suddenly seem to vanish only to land a few inches away, they are springing and they are indeed springtails.

On occasion another insect-like creature may be found which is not a springtail. If it is hard and brown with

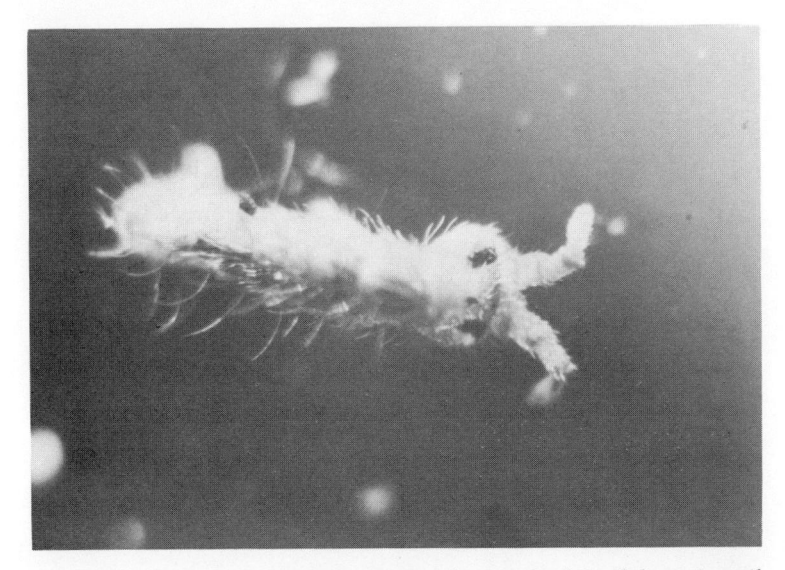

Illus. 79. A low-power photomicrograph reveals the adult springtail insect.

Illus. 80. The typical sort of soil beetle which appears in any growing environment, and is to be found in terraria.

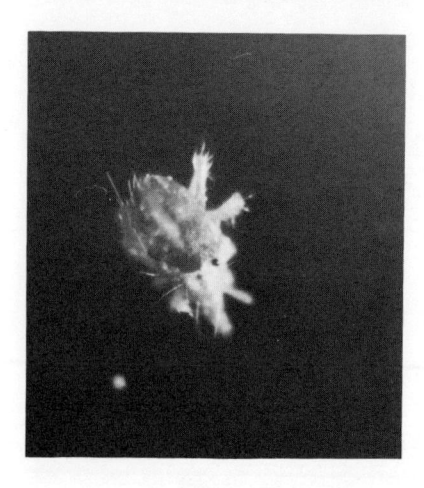

Illus. 81. The tiny plant mite is a relative of the spider and one of the most common of plant pests.

chunky segments and slightly larger than the springtail, it is a beetle, one of the many kinds that live in soil.

If you find a tiny insect-like organism with 8 legs it is a mite. Some of them, called red spiders, are very common on house plants, whose juices they suck through their long thin mouth parts. While rapid in their movements, mites are very interesting to watch.

There are many kinds of worms which grow in natural woodland soils. They range from the microscopic nematodes which are found nearly everywhere on earth to the common earthworm. While terrarium soil should be sterilized by heat before use, you can add a few small earthworms later and watch their growth and reproduction. They will tunnel to the surface and make castings just as they do in nature. These castings are one of the most

Illus. 82. An earthworm, the world's most valuable soil builder, crawls through its burrow.

concentrated of all fertilizers and can be collected in the woods for use in the terrarium. The animals of the terrarium must be kept in number and size so as to fit the tiny environment without destroying it. If the balance can be obtained it will yield a very interesting laboratory for the study of the interworkings of the woodland at large. In order to maintain the proper balance you must keep close watch on the animals and their activities. Reptiles and amphibians that grow too large should be removed to larger quarters. While toads and box turtles will eat some of the small insects that live on the terrarium

Illus. 83. The cast or manure of the earthworm is one of the richest fertilizers. Worms in terraria will produce these casts on the surface.

plants, these insects cannot be counted on as the sole source of food. The reptiles and amphibians will have to be fed additional rations on a regular basis. If the red spiders and white flies become too heavily encrusted on the plants, they should be washed off with a sponge.

8. History of Terraria

Millions of people crowded into London's magnificent Crystal Palace throughout the summer of 1851. They came from some 50 countries to attend the greatest world's fair of the time, the Exposition of the Industry of All Nations. Queen Victoria and Prince Albert visited the exposition to view the 15,000 inventions and devices on display. Three of the new inventions were especially popular with the visitors. They were the McCormick reaper, the first machine which could harvest grain; the Colt Repeating Pistol, a revolver which could fire six shots in quick succession; and the Wardian Case, the first terrarium.

The Wardian Case was named for its inventor, a British physician, Dr. Nathaniel Ward. He had discovered the principle of the terrarium by accident in autumn, 1829. Like many of the medical men of his time, Dr. Ward was interested in many different kinds of biology or what was called "Natural History" in the 19th century. He would often go on early morning walks around his London home. He was disturbed about the effects that smoke and dust,

Illus. 84. A woodland scene created in a large greenhouse to simulate nature. Note the rocks, water, mosses, ferns and small plants.

Illus. 85. The layout of a large terrarium includes mosses and lichens and a maidenhair fern in the deeper soil in the corner.

what we call air pollution, might have on the plants in gardens and parks.

On one of these walks he collected the hard case of a moth which was turning from a caterpillar into an adult. It was the chrysalis of a sphinx moth stuck to a hard clod of earth. He took it home and placed it into a glass jar with a tight lid so that he could watch the adult moth emerge. Shortly thereafter the sides of the glass jar began to show water droplets from the vapor collecting in the form of precipitation. Not long after, Dr. Ward noticed

Illus. 86. Small plants nestle against the sides of the glass to gain more sunlight.

two small green shoots emerging from the clod of earth. One was a fern and the other a blade of grass.

Ward was the son of a physician and a distinguished member of the Royal Society, England's special association of scientists. He was well aware of the experiments which had been carried on to try to discover the relationship of the gases in the air to the life processes of plants and animals.

Like all good scientists, Ward built his knowledge on the experiments of the scientists before him. He was very much interested in the problem of finding a "balance"

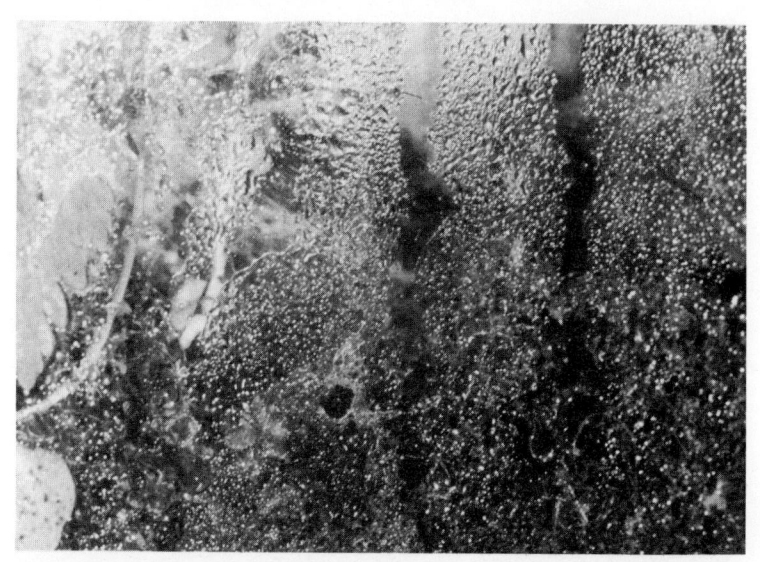

Illus. 87. The transpiration of the plants in a terrarium precipitates on the cooler glass as a constant area of water droplets.

between plants and animals which would allow each to provide for the other, what is today called a symbiotic relationship. After discovering the closed glass principle (that the plant could recycle its water), he proved that the trapped air in the enclosure also acted as insulation against sudden changes in temperature. Ward was able to keep ferns growing in unopened cases or what we would call closed terraria for up to four years. He published his discoveries in the botanical journals of the time. His invention was put to important and immediate use.

Illus. 88. A successful terrarium makes use of many kinds of mosses.

In 1833, Ward sent two of his cases to Sydney, Australia with ferns from England. The ferns survived the months of hard travel at sea and the cases were returned to him with plants from Australia which survived the journey through the icy waters off the tip of South America and the terrible heat of the Equator. Three years later, various writers began to describe the Wardian Case and in 1838, John Williams used Ward's invention to transport the Chinese banana plant from the botanical gardens at Chatsworth in England to the far-off islands of Samoa in the south-central Pacific. Two years later another

Illus. 89. A small fern grows among rich humus and a small patch of lichens.

famous traveller, George Pritchard, used the Wardian Case to take the same banana plant to two other Pacific island countries, Fiji and Tonga. Wardian Cases were used in 1845 to transport 20,000 tea plants from Shanghai, China to the Himalayas of India and thereafter to transplant the chinchona tree and its medical use to cure malaria from China to India. While we do not think much about the Wardian Case or terrarium as a great invention today, it was used to add enormous new supplies of food and medicine to overcrowded areas of the world.

Dr. Nathaniel Ward published a detailed description of

his invention and experiments in a book titled, *On the Growth of Plants in Closely Glazed Cases* in 1842. Within a decade, every upper class Victorian home had its elaborate wrought-iron Wardian Case filled with ferns and bog plants. However, the Wardian Case served a much more serious scientific purpose because it provided a tiny laboratory in which scientists could observe closely the development and processes of plants and animals. Ward discovered the principle of gaseous balance for which chemists and biologists had sought. Even though Ward worked mostly with earth in his glass cases, he was also interested in aquarium life and applied his insights to plants and fishes in aquaria. His work was the pioneering research into balanced aquaria. His views of the exchange of gases in his cases were also correct when applied to the watery medium.

The term Wardian Cases was used for many years after Ward's death in 1868. However, another word, analogous to "aquarium" was used in the French botanical literature beginning in 1873 and first appeared in English in 1895. This was the word "terrarium." The most popular form was a large bell-shaped jar placed over a plant pot or plant box. Some larger terraria were built up to 9 square feet (0.85 m.^{2}) and often animals such as salamanders and turtles were kept with the plants. A new term was proposed for these mixed plant-animal environments and they were sometimes called "vivaria" after the Latin word *vivus*, meaning alive. This term was used throughout the

Illus. 90. A large brass-framed terrarium, the classical Victorian Wardian Case, is filled with woodland plants.

last decades of the 19th century and up until the 1930's in the United States but both types of enclosures are now simply called terraria.

INDEX

algae, 45–47
angiosperms, 65, 67, 69, 70–71
animals suitable for terraria, 74–82
  anole, 74, 75
  box turtle, 75, 76, 81, 82
  insects, 76–82
  toad, 74, 75, 81, 82
  worms, 80, 81
antagonism, 44
autotrophic, 45
balance
  between plants and animals, 86, 87
  in terrarium, 81, 82
balanced plant-animal community principle, 73
biome, 7, 27
"bottle gardens," 11
buttercup family, 44
cactus, 5, 26, 28
carnivorous plants, 69
castings, 80, 81
cellulose, 33
"chameleon," 75
chlorophyll, 41
climate, 27–34
closed glass principle, 87
communities, 41
containers, 7, 11–12
  cleaning of, 13
croziers, 57
Crystal Palace, 83
deciduous trees, 29
desiccation, 33
dwarfing, 36–37

energy, 41–42
epiphytes, 42, 43
exotic plants, 45, 67
Exposition of the Industry of All Nations, 83
ferns, 57–64
fertilizers, 25, 81
fission, 46
freezing, 38
fungi, 47–48
fungi terrarium, 48–49
gametophyte, 53, 54, 61
greenhouse, 6, 8–10
hormones, 47
horsetails, 63, 64
horticultural halls, 10
humus, 14, 16, 30, 33
hyphae, 47
insect infestation, 24
lichens, 34, 35, 42, 48–53
light, 24–25, 35–37
  diffused light, 36
  suffused light, 37
micro-organisms, 15
moss garden, 8, 13
mosses, 53–56
moulds, 13, 25, 47
mushrooms, 47
"Natural History", 83
On the Growth of Plants in Closely Glazed Cases, 90
orchids, 28, 29
photosynthesis, 25, 51, 55
plant-animal interdependence, 73

planting, 16–23
plants, types of
  desert, 26–28
  rain-forest, 28–29
  woodlands, 29–33
Priestley, Joseph, 73
Pritchard, George, 89
radiation, 41
reproduction, 46, 47, 52, 55, 56, 57
rhizomes, 70
Royal Society, 86
saprophytes, 47, 49
seasonal cycle, 38
self-watering, 38, 40
soil, preparation of, 15–26
sori, 60, 61
sporedia, 52
spores, 56, 61, 63
sporophyte, 61
sun-dew, 69
symbionts, 49, 50, 51
symbiosis, 42, 49, 57, 87
synergism, 42
temperature, 35, 38
thalli, 50, 52
transpiration, 39, 40, 87
tree seedlings, 71, 72
trimming, 24, 37
Venus's fly-trap, 69
violet, 65
"vivaria," 90
Ward, Nathaniel, and Wardian Case (first terrarium), 73, 83, 85–91
washing of plants, 24
watering, 23–24
Williams, John, 88

DATE DUE

29 Feb 77			
19 Apr 77			
11 Oct 78			
31 Jan 81			
17 Nov 81			
NOV 17 1981			
11 Dec 81			
SE 27 '90			
APR 1 0 2001			

GAYLORD — PRINTED IN U.S.A.

TVSNA11378C